GOLD
and
Other
Precious
Metals

GOLD
and Other Precious Metals

CHARLES COOMBS

illustrated with photographs

William Morrow and Company
New York   1981

Library of Congress Cataloging in Publication Data

Coombs, Charles Ira, 1914–
    Gold and other precious metals.
    Includes index.
    Summary: Discusses the desirable properties and uses of gold, silver, and platinum; describes the nineteenth-century gold rush; discusses techniques of mining and refining gold; and presents an amateur's guide for gold prospecting.
    1. Gold—Juvenile literature. 2. Precious metals—Juvenile literature. [1. Gold. 2. Gold mines and mining. 3. Precious metals] I. Title.
TN420.C66   669'.22   81-38414
ISBN 0-688-00542-X   AACR2
ISBN 0-688-00543-8 (lib. bdg.)

Photo Credits

All photographs are by the author with the exception of the following: Allis-Chalmers Corp., pp. 48, 50, 51, 117; Armand Hammer Foundation, p. 17; Bancroft Library, p. 44; California State Library, pp. 33, 42, 43; Eastman Kodak Company, p. 115; Engelhard Industries, pp. 19, 95, 96, 98, 106; General Motors, pp. 119 (both); Gold Information Center, pp. 97, 102, 105; Gold King Mfg., Inc., p. 72; Handy & Harman, p. 109; Homestake Mining Company, pp. 38 bottom, 52, 54, 55; Hughes Aerospace, p. 101; Keene Engineering, pp. 31, 87, 90; Kennecott Minerals Company (Don Green, photographer), pp. 15, 111, 112, 113; Stewart Library of Western Americana, p. 39; Tuolumne County Historical Society, p. 26; U.S. Bureau of Mines, pp. 62, 75; U.S. Department of the Interior, pp. 110, 116; U.S. Geological Survey, p. 34. Permission is gratefully acknowledged.

Contents

c.1

Foreword

Preparing for and writing this book has been both fun and a real challenge. The search for gold, or other valued metal, lies somewhere deep in the Coombs' family veins. Some years ago my brother and I inherited two placer claims staked out by our adventuresome father. The claims—twenty acres each—are located near Quartzsite, deep in the hot, but beautiful Arizona desert.

When my brother and I took over the claims, we knew very little about mining. But we tried to become miners, and we gained experience. Dad had built a dry washer according to plans undoubtedly dug out of some government publication or provided by the Bureau of Mines, United States Department of the Interior. We used it, and at times we still sweat over it.

Recently, though, we have "gone modern" and begun to use a sensitive electronic metal detector. Although "sweeping" forty acres with an eight-inch disk, or loop, takes a long time, we're in no hurry. The excitement and expectation of the hunt are a big part of the treasure.

Perhaps that is fortunate. Thus far we have not been able to find enough gold (or silver, platinum, or lead, for that matter) to "prove up." Consequently, we have never been able to patent our claims—that is, get full title to the land by virtue of finding "commercially valuable" minerals.

We are still prospecting. Each year, when weather permits, we trek out to Quartzsite to do our assessment work as the Government requires. We paint the trim on the old cabin that Dad built stone by stone. We clean the well and repair the dirt road washed out by seasonal cloudbursts.

We dig, we dry wash, and we listen to the soft murmurs and promising sputters of a battery-powered detector. I would love to be able to say that we have a Mason jar full of nuggets. Not so.

But there is always the hope. Down this arroyo, over that rise, along the desert wash, or clinging to the roots of some gnarled saguaro cactus may be our bonanza, just waiting to be discovered.

If not, perhaps another trip to the Mother Lode— I haven't yet tried the metal detector there—may sniff out a fortune. Frankly, I'd settle for a pea-sized nugget and cherish it as fervently as a nation cherishes its crown jewels.

In fact, when you get right down to it, the size of the nugget or, indeed, whether or not there even is a nugget has little to do with the real pleasure of prospecting. The biggest treasure is the joy and anticipation of the search itself. And the knowledge that goes with it. At least, that is my experience.

Perhaps this book will interest you in trying your own treasure hunts for one of the precious metals.

Charles "Chick" Coombs
Westlake Village, California 1981

1

Precious Metals

Eons ago, as this planet began to cool and harden, certain chemical elements separated from its molten core and squeezed outward into the rocky pores of Earth's crust. These elements are known as metals. They share certain characteristics and differ greatly in others. Most, but not all, are silvery white in color. All but a few are heavier than water. Some are brittle and break easily. Some can be drawn out thin or hammered flat without shattering. Most are good conductors of heat and electricity. Many can be mixed

13

together to form alloys that are stronger and better than the separate metals.

There are about eighty different metals—from aluminum through nickel to zinc. A few common alloys such as brass and bronze are often considered metals in themselves. Some metals, like iron, tin, and copper, are well known and widely used. Others, like cerium, dysprosium, and thulium are little known and little used.

Metals are divided into two main categories—base and precious. The base, or common, metals form by far the larger group and include such familiar elements as copper, iron, lead, mercury, nickel, tin, and zinc, plus many lesser-known metals. Important as they are, most common metals are either so soft, so hard, or so brittle that their use is limited unless they are combined with other elements to improve their characteristics. The most common fault of the base metals is that they tend to break down under exposure to other nonmetallic elements. They rust and corrode or otherwise deteriorate when they come in contact with the alkalis and acids that are everywhere in nature.

Nevertheless, base metals form the major building blocks of the world. Without iron, copper, tin, lead, and others, present-day civilization could not have developed.

On the other hand, there is a select small group of rare and highly valued metals whose appeal and matchless qualities make them superior to and more valuable than the common metals. They are the precious metals —silver, platinum, and gold. They are strong, they resist the corrosion that causes base metals to weaken,

Seventy-pound silver ingots ready for shipment to various arts and industry customers.

and they are soft and malleable so they can be drawn out thin, hammered, or shaped without crushing or shattering.

Silver, which carries the chemical symbol *Ag*, from the Latin name *argentum*, is a moonbeam-colored metal that was known to and first used by primitive man. He dug it from the ground or found it lying about; polished it to a lustrous, eye-appealing shine; and shaped it into ornaments to please the gods. Later he fashioned it into useful utensils such as pots, plates, and goblets and decorated his weapons with it.

Platinum (chemical symbol *Pt*), on the other hand, was not even identified as a metal until around the midsixteenth century. Then it was not put to practical use for another two hundred years. An extremely heavy, steel-gray metal, platinum weighs about twenty-one times as much as water, heavier even than gold. It can be worked and shaped almost as readily as the other two precious metals and is highly resistant to corrosion. The least plentiful of the three, platinum also is the most costly. However, neither its rarity nor high price make it the most desirable metal.

Gold has that rank. It is by far the world's most sought-after metal. With its lustrous, never-fading yellow sheen, its pleasing feel, and its unmatched versatility and durability, gold has long been the king of metals. Jewelers favor it for creating masterworks of craftsmanship; men and women wear it to enhance their appearance. Golden artifacts, unfaded throughout the centuries, aid the archaeologist in tracing the course of history from Egyptian tombs to Inca ruins. The absolute reliability and permanence of gold make it ideal for use in many areas of modern industry.

For its beauty, strength, and versatility, gold, indeed, is unmatched by any other of Earth's metallic elements.

A fourteenth-century miniature mask and breastplate typifies the work of early Mexican goldsmiths.

Recent diggings along the Bulgarian coast of the Black Sea have turned up jewelry and gold artifacts dating to about 4000 B.C. Early Egyptians and Greeks made delicate gold chains and ornaments for their hair. The Romans carved gold bracelets and rings and set them with gems. They called the gleaming metal *aurum*, from which gold's chemical symbol, *Au*, derives. The early Etruscans of Italy, the Aztecs of Mexico, the Incas of Peru, and natives of other lands fashioned necklaces, earrings, and other treasures from gold they had dug or traded.

The Bible abounds in stories of gold and its uses. And religious objects such as scepters and chalices were, and still are, largely crafted of gleaming gold inlaid with precious stones.

Throughout history, gold has been ever present. Knights rode into battle while tugging gold-handled swords from gold-encrusted scabbards. Kings and noblemen of all nations at one time or another drank their wine from solid gold goblets and ate from golden dishes. Gold has been a favorite setting for the crown jewels of most countries. Many of these objects are displayed in palaces and museums throughout the world for all to see and marvel at.

Gold coins were crudely minted as far back as 560 B.C. by Croesus, king of Lydia (now Turkey), known for his immense wealth. Not surprisingly, gold became a popular medium of barter and a symbol of wealth and power. Peoples migrated around the world searching for it. Because of gold they explored new territories. Dutch colonists settled in South Africa. Spaniards sailed the seas to plunder the gold of Mexico and Peru. Some stayed. In a later time, the westward gold rush changed the face of the United States.

In the modern world, the value of gold increased and declined according to its availability and the economy of the times. Gold became so important a commodity that for a while some nations went on a gold standard. They issued paper money that, should the holder wish, he or she could redeem for gold. The price of gold was set so they could trade among themselves on a fixed level. Nonmember countries were

Pure gold ingots help support the world's wealth and industry.

forced into other means of barter, not usually to their advantage.

In time, however, more gold certificates were being issued than there was gold to back them up. In 1934, the United States dropped the gold standard and recalled all gold from circulation. Other nations made similar changes, and today no country remains on a gold standard.

In an effort to control gold further, the Government of the United States prohibited private ownership of it from 1934 to 1968. There was no objection to a person having a few items of jewelry or retaining long-held artifacts. But to buy or hoard pure gold was against the law. Interest in gold, particularly in the search for it, further waned when the price per ounce was frozen at the very low figure of $35.

Unable to make a fair profit, mines closed down and prospectors tossed away their picks and shovels. Although gold still was in demand for both arts and industry, the effort and cost of finding and digging it simply was not worth the final reward. The search for gold reached an all-time low.

Then, slowly at first, the situation began to change. In 1968, the price freeze of $35 an ounce for gold was lifted. Yet, during the next few years, the price of gold edged only slightly upward. But, in 1974, the price

20

increased suddenly when there were strong indications that the Government was about to relax its regulations. Gold began to sell for as high as $160 an ounce. Prospectors dusted off their gold pans and visited land offices to see what public properties were still available for staking claims.

And, indeed, on January 1, 1975, the United States officially rescinded the ban on private ownership of gold. Once again gold could be freely and legally owned and traded.

In anticipation of its sudden rise in price, a whole new generation of eager prospectors returned to the long-abandoned goldfields. They swarmed along rocky stream beds, dug into mountain slopes, and sifted

Elbow-to-elbow prospectors crowd along
a promising stretch of a graveled stream.

desert sands in search of the increasingly precious yellow metal.

Suddenly, in the spring of 1980, the price of gold skyrocketed to well over $800 an ounce. Despite the fact that it soon settled back down to around $500 an ounce, the price was still more than ample to maintain the momentum of the search.

A new gold rush was under way.

2

The Rush for Gold

Early generations of Americans were much interested in the search for gold. They had heard tales of native Indians adorning themselves with the gleaming metal long before the Europeans arrived. They knew of the vast golden riches that had been stolen by Spanish conquerors as they looked for the fabled Seven Cities of Cibola. Rumors of gold persisted around farm and fireside.

Then, about the year 1800, minor gold discoveries were made in North Carolina. Appetites for the precious metal were quickly whetted. By 1830, prospectors made additional strikes in Georgia, Alabama, and other Southern states. Moving westward, some prospectors turned up gold dust and small nuggets around New Mexico. All were modest discoveries.

Finally the big bonanza appeared. It arrived on the morning of January 24, 1848, in the small backwoods settlement of Coloma, located along the American River in northern California. James Marshall, a newcomer to the West, was inspecting the tailrace that led away from the waterwheel that powered the small sawmill he had just built for his employer, Captain John Sutter. In his own words, Marshall said that as his eyes grew accustomed to the early-morning light, he "caught a glimpse of something shining in the bottom of the ditch. It was only about half the size of a pea, worth perhaps fifty cents, if it was really gold, not iron pyrite, known as fool's gold."

Marshall placed the small yellow particle on a river stone and hammered it with a rock. It did not shatter as brittle fool's gold would but flattened out, still in one piece. Eureka! It was true gold!

Despite attempts to keep the secret, the news quickly leaked out. Spurred more by rumor of limitless wealth than by fact, the California gold rush began.

Doctors, lawyers, merchants, wagon masters, sales-

The author at Sutter's Mill, where it all began.

men, farmers, preachers, and sheepherders packed up their belongings and headed west "to see the elephant," a term given to their blind desire to join in the massive search for gold, whatever the hardships. The headlong migration was unstoppable. Along the eastern seaboard thousands of modern-day Argonauts, not unlike the followers of the mythical Greek prince Jason, set out in ships to search for the Golden Fleece. The forty-niners were drawn by rumors of egg-sized

The California gold rush attracted people from all walks of life.

golden nuggets said to lie ankle-deep along the rivers and streams of California's Mother Lode in the north-central part of what was soon to become the nation's thirty-first state.

Ill-advised about the rigors of the journey, the fortune hunters boarded vessels of all sizes and shapes to embark on a thirteen-thousand-mile voyage from New York or Boston around the tip of South America and up the Pacific coast to the California goldfields. At best, the voyage took several months; at worst, more than a year. The violent Cape Horn weather took its toll of ships and human lives. Contaminated food and disease incapacitated many of the Argonauts.

To shorten the treacherous trip, numerous ships unloaded their passengers on the Atlantic side of the Isthmus of Panama. There the westbound pilgrims set out upon the relatively short but highly perilous over-land journey through the jungles and fever-ridden swamps of the isthmus to the Pacific shore. Those who survived boarded waiting ships for the remainder of the journey north. That many made it—thousands didn't, but tens of thousands did—now seems amazing.

Other hopeful prospectors set out across the prairies from the banks of the Mississippi and Missouri Rivers. Some joined wagon trains. Others traveled afoot, carrying tools and supplies on their backs. Indeed, a few ambitious but misguided souls stacked their worldly goods onto wheelbarrows and moved doggedly westward, lucky if their strength held out a day or two.

Many overlanders were attacked by Indians, who had long been mistreated and had little choice but to try and stem the threat of the new migrations. Hundreds more died of thirst or starvation. Cholera took a heavy toll. Others, on the eve of success, perished in the winter snows of the Sierra Mountains. Bone weary and beset by grueling, unanticipated hardships, many forty-niners halfway into their overland journey looked up aghast at the towering Rocky Mountains blocking their path to California. Thousands gave up, turned around, and went back home without ever seeing the elephant.

Despite all these obstacles, the goldfields of California soon swarmed with prospectors of all races and cultures. There were Yankees, Kentuckians, Midwestern farmers, and Americans from every state and territory. Thousands of eager prospectors trekked northward from Mexico. Others came from France, Germany, Chile, Australia, China, and from nearly every other part of the world. Some came overland, but most arrived by ship in San Francisco. Without pause, as soon as they put ashore, they shouldered their packs and proceeded a hundred miles inland. San Francisco Bay was jammed with deserted ships.

All had a single aim—get to the gold and load up before it ran out. Gold was found, although far too little to satisfy most of the seekers. Bonanzas were few and far between. Grim lessons were quickly and painfully learned.

When a rare egg-sized nugget turned up in someone's gold pan, an entire new town might spring up overnight. Made up of tents and crude wood shanties, it had stores, hotels, wagon shops, livery stables, assay offices, sawmills, and saloons. Even churches. It catered to every miner's need, good or bad. It was called Hangtown, Volcano, Poker Flat, Rough and Ready, Fiddletown, Angels Camp, or Bedbug. With prices in the Mother Lode inflated beyond all reason, the butchers, bartenders, shopkeepers, and boardinghouse cooks usually were far more prosperous than the miners.

Fire took a heavy toll of the flimsy, hastily built shantytowns. One day's lively settlement became the next day's smouldering ash heap. Often low-lying gold towns were flooded out by high waters of the spring runoffs. Some towns were quickly rebuilt; others simply were abandoned, as merchants and miners set out for new locations of real or rumored riches.

But, despite the hardships and broken dreams, the forty-niners persisted in their search. They sifted the sands and gravels of every likely stream or dry gully that wound through the pine-forested mountains and brush-covered hills of central and northern California. They started with their shallow, slope-sided steel pans. Filling them with promising material, the miners flipped aside the stones and sloshed out the soil and lighter materials to get down to that spoonful or so of heavy black sand, always searching hopefully through it for a pinch of yellow dust or, even better, a gleaming golden nugget.

Some succeeded. Many nuggets appeared in pans, and even an occasional supernugget weighing fifteen or twenty pounds turned up at the end of a pick. But a great many did not succeed. Fortunate, indeed, were those who, by the end of a long week's work, had enough dust in their pokes to replenish their supply of pork, beans, coffee, and flour. Potatoes at a dollar a pound were beyond most budgets. An ounce of gold, at the going price of about $16, might buy a pound of raisins for a fruit-starved miner threatened with scurvy. But it would not buy a pick, a blanket, or a dozen eggs.

Still, during the bonanza years from 1849 to 1851, millions of dollars' worth of the precious metal was

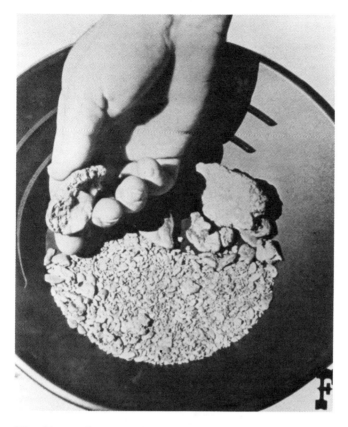

The Forty-niners used shallow, slope-sided steel pans
in their search for gleaming nuggets of gold.

gleaned from stream beds or hillside terraces that
marked ancient waterways in the Mother Lode. Much
more was panned in the rich Grass Valley area a bit
farther north. It appeared as pinches of dust, small
golden grains, and nuggets of all sizes.

Whatever its form or size, this gold was called
"placer" gold, from a Spanish word that referred to

water-eroded gold that had chipped off the end of some protruding vein of ore and was washed down into canyons and stream beds. This free, or loose, gold was just waiting to be panned.

The forty-niners, however, soon became impatient with the slow process of panning. Quickly they developed faster methods for separating gold from the large volumes of waste material in which it was found.

In order to increase production, the prospectors built rockers. Generally three-foot-long and cradle-like, these contraptions handled many times the amount of sand and gravel that could be panned. From the rocker evolved the so-called long tom. This device was simply an inclined trough a dozen or so feet long. It had slats, or riffles, tacked across the bottom to trap the heavy gold as it dropped out of the flow. The next logical step was to make still longer troughs, called "sluices." They might extend for hundreds of feet and require a dozen or so men to shovel and stir the sand and gravel into the stream of water that flowed along their entire length.

Still later the prospectors employed hydraulics to handle even larger quantities of gold-bearing sand and gravel. They piped water from high in the hills to build up pressure. Spurting it through giant nozzles, called "monitors," they washed away entire hills. They

Miners operated long sluices to wash gold
out of the earth's overburden.

channeled the muddy slurry through meandering riffle-bottomed sluices to settle out the gold. These hydraulic monitors laid waste to the land and polluted streams. But they processed a large volume of material and so turned up considerable golden riches, which was all anyone really was concerned about at the time.

Never quite satisfied, the miners built large floating dredges with endless chains of buckets that chewed

Giant gold dredges chewed their way across the landscape.

across the flatlands. The dredges sifted through tons of sand and stones for a single ounce of precious gold. Sometimes the dredge followed an established river-bed. At other times it started operating on a small man-made pond. As it gnawed its way forward, sorting through the pay dirt, it cast the useless tailings behind it to fill in the excavation. Thus, it moved the pond right along with it and thereby kept afloat.

So, by means of both simple and ingeniously complex methods, most stream beds and hillsides of the Mother Lode and Grass Valley areas were worked over and over again. Every reachable crack and crevice was probed with fingernail or knife blade. Nuggets that might have settled there a million or more years ago were pried out and carefully tucked away.

And when the more eager prospectors were satisfied that they had gotten all there was to get, they moved on. After them, the more patient Chinese arrived to rework the diggings and, indeed, sometimes found their own small fortunes.

But by early in the 1850s, for most practical purposes, the easy-to-reach placer gold of California was gone. Still, the dream of riches was as vivid and tempting as ever. Whereas the loose placer gold had been worked out, miners believed that somewhere deep underground lay the main deposits from which the surface gold had broken off ages earlier. They also believed that all one needed to do was dig down into the granite and quartz, in which most gold seemed to originate, find a vein or pocket, and pry out new wealth.

It was time to go underground in search of riches.

3

Hardrock Mining

Hardrock, or deep-shaft mining involved different tools and different skills from those used in placer mining. The exploratory geology, the purchase of equipment, the large-scale dynamiting, digging, and removal of ore required a large work force and cost a great deal of money. The prospector with large hopes but a small pan or rocker was ill equipped for deep mining.

Thus, most profitable hardrock mines were company owned and operated. Dozens of such mines appeared all over northern California. Towering headframes

Then and now—
above, a headframe and ghostly buildings of an early hardrock
mine stand beyond the remnants of a tailing wheel;
below, the towering headframe of a large, modern hardrock mine,
surrounded by a variety of gold-processing structures.

arose over ever-deepening shafts being hollowed into the earth. These headframes contained the pulleys and hoisting gear needed to transport miners and equipment into and out of the shafts and to bring out the ore. Other support buildings housed pumps, ore crushers, ventilation systems, and processing facilities.

A different breed of man was needed to work the

Hardrock miners had to go deep into the earth to reach gold.

deep mines. Usually the placer miners disdained the idea of laboring long hours, sweating in the dank underground for small wages and no real share of the profits. They stuck to their pans and sluices as long as possible. Thus, many companies imported hardrock miners from the coalfields of Wales. Also boatloads of Englishmen arrived from Cornwall. There were Poles, Swedes, Austrians, and Italians. Even without speaking each other's language, they knew mining techniques and were hard workers.

Meanwhile, many disgruntled placer miners packed up their picks and pans and migrated eastward over the towering Sierras. They fanned out into Nevada, Arizona, Utah, Colorado, Wyoming, New Mexico— wherever traces of pay dirt could be found. Others trekked northward into Oregon and Washington, where a few gold strikes had been made. Many of the Argonauts took to the seas again, heading for Australia, where gold was rumored to lie handy to anyone willing to stoop and pick it up. Indeed, such rumors, fortified by occasional rich strikes, redistributed people to many parts of the world.

Although there were still plenty of deep quartz mines paying off in the Mother Lode and Grass Valley areas of California, a major exodus from these worked-over goldfields had taken place by 1859. In that year, the bonanza of all bonanzas was uncovered on the forested slope of Mount Davidson in the Nevada Territory. Part of the Washoe Range, Mount Davidson raises its peak well east of the high Sierras and looks down into the lush valley of the Carson River. Its rugged sides and steep canyons had been halfheartedly explored years earlier by prospectors hurriedly passing through on their way to the Mother Lode. Indeed, a small amount of gold had been panned there. But the forty-niners had difficulty separating the gold-bearing pay dirt from the mysterious, heavy bluish muck in which it was so often mixed.

One day, however, several men, including Henry Comstock, located a small gold vein poking from atop a deserted knoll, which they logically named Gold Hill. As they dug deeper into the mountain, the vein widened out. It was not placer gold but a solid underground deposit, or lode. Still, there was that bluish sandy muck to contend with. One of the miners, curious why most of the gold seemed mixed in with the troublesome stuff, sacked up a good-sized sample of it, saddled up a mule, and headed across the Sierras to show it to a reputable assayer over in Grass Valley.

El Dorado! The sample proved rich beyond belief. The gold itself assayed out at nearly $900 to a ton of ore—an amazingly profitable ratio. But, in addition,

Giant tailing wheels and flumes carried waste
away from a mining operation.

the bothersome blue muck turned out to be almost
pure silver. In that particular sample, the silver alone
was worth nearly $3,000 per ton!

The unbelievably rich Comstock Lode had been
discovered. In no time at all, the land on and around

Mount Davidson was completely staked out with claim notices. New shafts were sunk almost daily into the rich ore. Mine buildings sprouted everywhere. Because he needed a mailing address, one homesick miner from Dixie started to call the burgeoning new town Virginia City. The name stuck.

Soon the entire area was honeycombed with shafts

Mule-drawn wagons hauled Virginia City ore to a refinery.

Comstock miners worked the rich gold lode
room by timbered room.

and tunnels. So rich were some of the gold- and silver-ore pockets that fortunes were often made by miners who were able to lay claim to only a few square feet of surface area.

Most mining of the Comstock, however, was left to the big corporations that were financed and equipped to operate on a large scale. They, too, were the outfits capable of handling the added complication of processing the silver that, in fact, comprised more than half of the total production of the Comstock.

The fabulous Comstock continued to produce vast quantities of gold and silver for more than twenty-five years. Pocket after pocket was exposed. Small veins led to richer veins. Millions of dollars' worth of gold and silver ore were hoisted up from the steaming depths and refined into yellow and gray bars of bullion.

And then the earth started to move as hastily dug and improperly shored tunnels caved in. Men died beneath the ground, and buildings cracked and crumbled on the surface.

An even more dangerous problem was the flooding of the mines by underground water. The straining steam-powered pumps could no longer handle it. Workers dug a tunnel out the side of the mountain to form a drain. But it, too, was soon overwhelmed by the torrents of water rising from deep down where age-old smoldering subterranean fires heated it almost to a boil. Although some Comstock mines continued to produce well into the twentieth century, most of them had to be abandoned.

In time, the last of nearly one hundred mine shafts in the area was closed off. Virginia City turned into a ghost town of crumbling buildings and rusting mine machinery. However, before the famous Comstock Lode slipped quietly into history, it had produced some $400,000,000 in silver and gold. Never before or since has there been a strike in the United States to match its richness.

But hardrock miners around the world kept searching for new bonanzas. At the time, Russia was producing vast amounts of gold, little of which was allowed to leave the country. Mines that had started operating in South Africa around 1870 expanded underground until they were producing more than half of the gold needed in the West. In the early 1900s, both the Canadian Yukon territory and Alaska had substantial gold rushes. Although the search surged and dwindled, it never really stopped.

Yet, by the early 1940s, the low price of gold, the rapidly increasing costs of operation, and the frequent cave-ins and floodings had closed most of the deep mines in the United States. Only a very few survived the material and manpower shortages caused by World War II. The fabulous Homestake Mine in South Dakota was one of those allowed to continue operating and soon became the United States' major gold producer.

In recent years, however, many old mines have been pumped out, retimbered, restored, and put back to work. Efficient electric power has replaced the water, steam, or mule power of earlier days. But only those mines that can pass inspection and be worked safely have been allowed to reopen. Some new mines have been established.

Improved recovery and refining technologies, coupled with the continuing high price of gold, sometimes make profitable the reworking of millions of tons of tailings that were once discarded as worthless by-products of an earlier mining operation. In a process called "heap leaching," a weak cyanide solution is filtered through finely ground mine rubble or low-grade ore. The cyanide dissolves and draws out the gold. The solution is collected and the gold extracted by adding zinc, which precipitates out the gold.

Mercury or carbon are sometimes added to the mud-like ore slurry to absorb the precious metal and form a spongy mass. The sponge is then refined to separate out the gold, which is converted into bars of bullion.

Still another practical process for separating gold or other desired metals is called "froth flotation." Again, the finely crushed ore is mixed into a souplike solution. Then air is pumped into it, forming billions of tiny bubbles. Although some of the gold settles to the bottom of the tank, most of it attaches to the bubbles and rises to the surface, where it is skimmed off. The ore may go through several flotation stages before complete recovery of the desired metals is achieved.

Now many modern hardrock mines, both large and

Batteries of froth flotation cells separate
the gold from the mudlike ore.

small, are turning a profit and helping to meet the demand for precious metals.

But hardrock mining poses problems not present in surface operations. As a mine shaft sinks ever deeper into the earth, the temperature steadily increases. In very deep mines, intricate and expensive air-conditioning systems must be installed to provide miners with fresh air and protect them from the heat. This installation becomes a major task in mines that may reach a mile or more underground. At best, most deep-shaft miners work in an oppressively hot and damp atmosphere.

Another hazard is that rock pressures increase with increasing mine depth. Tunneling into the rock can release the stress, and the solid granite or quartz sometimes literally explodes. So great care must be taken when excavating tunnels and shoring up the walls and ceilings.

Dust and mechanical problems constantly plague the miners. Spraying down the dust and wearing face masks that filter the air are measures that help protect miners from developing silicosis, a crippling lung disease.

Underground mining also involves the process of crushing and transporting the ore to a refinery, which requires costly equipment and procedures.

A giant whirling grinding mill converts chunks
of gold-bearing ore into a fine powder.

Many different kinds of workers are essential to the
operation of a deep mine. Engineers, carpenters,
plumbers, electricians, drillers, blasters, mechanics,
truckers, and cooks are all necessary. But the hardest

Giant crushers pulverize the mined ore.

and most exacting tasks fall to the miners who go underground.

Dressed in coveralls, heavy boots, hard hats, and usually carrying lunch pails, the miners descend in

Underground miners work in dank areas of potential danger.

rattling cages deep into the earth. Often they are lowered a mile or so underground. Guided by the miner's lights attached to their hard hats, they work a rich seam that may be either a few inches or several feet thick. If the seam holds out, everybody profits. The miners, who work in teams, frequently get paid according to a bonus system. The harder they work and the more they produce, the more they earn. So a widening vein means prosperity, while a pinched-out one brings disappointment.

First the miners drill a series of holes about ten feet into the working face of the mine. Sometimes there is enough room to work standing up. At other times, they kneel or squat at their task. At best, they will be sore and sweaty during most of their eight-hour shift. After packing the holes with explosives, the powder men string several hundred feet of blasting wire around some safe corner where they will be protected from flying rock. They attach the wires to a detonator, sound a warning, and push the button.

After the dust from the explosion settles, the muckers return to the working face to load the loose rock into ore cars that transport it to the surface. Modern mines usually use electric-powered trams instead of the old mule-drawn cars.

As the rooms, or stopes, in which the miners work

Drilling blasting holes in an underground stope
is hard, noisy work.

increase in size, special teams bolt steel plates to walls
and ceilings to prevent cave-ins. Or they use heavy
timber props. Thus, a large hardrock mine continues
to expand underground just as long as there is a seam

to follow and pay dirt to bring out. The vertical shafts deepen, and the lateral tunnels, or drifts, spread out in spider-web fashion, always following a rich vein or searching for a new one.

One mining method backfills the stope after the gold-bearing ore is removed.

gold ore

slusher

6" sand-cement cap

sand backfill

sand backfill

chimney

caps

gob fence

10"-square wood blocks

rock

sand backfill

CUT-AND-FILL STOPE

Modern miners pay extremely close attention to safety factors that in early days were too often slighted. A large mine spreads out like an underground city with its streetlike network of passages leading to mineral-rich stopes. A mine has depotlike stations at various levels for handling the ore. It has a sophisticated communications system for keeping everyone above and below in constant contact.

Miners give careful attention to the safety of the underground electrical system that supplies both lighting and power to the operation. Electricity maintains the controlled environment. It operates the pumps that usually work continuously to prevent water seepage from flooding out the mine. It runs the machines.

Mining machinery that chews and crushes hard ore is usually very noisy. With some success, efforts have been made to dampen and insulate the sound. Miners also wear ear plugs or more sophisticated sound suppressors. But the sheer racket that goes with operating a mine remains a health hazard in some areas, and methods of control are constantly being worked on and improved.

Fire prevention is an essential part of underground mining. Fire can occur in a gold or silver mine almost as readily as in a coal mine. Combustible subterranean gases collect in any improperly ventilated mine. A spark can set mine timbers afire. An electrical short can start a blaze. Miners are trained to prevent these hazards if possible and to fight them should prevention fail.

Hardrock miners constantly check for seepage of poisonous gas that sometimes collects in underground formations. And they practice rapid and systematic evacuation of the mine whenever concentrations of any dangerous gas collect.

First-aid supplies are placed strategically throughout the mine, and every miner is carefully trained in their use. Thus, today's hardrock miners are about as secure as anyone can be in a job that is inherently hazardous.

Miners labor in one of the world's dirtiest, most difficult, most dangerous jobs. Yet they have their satisfactions. Most of them are proud of their activities deep underground while scratching precious metals out of the earth's stubbornly resisting rock.

4

The Search

The search for gold certainly is not confined to professional miners or corporations. The lure of the precious metal has beckoned to generations of eager amateurs. In recent years, the appeal has been heightened by the greatly increased value of gold.

Consequently, during recent years, hordes of amateur prospectors, young and old, have taken to searching the hillsides, creek beds, and desert wastes wherever "colors," bits of gold, have been discovered at one time or another. Armed with gold pan, sluice, dredge, or

Modern prospectors shop for equipment
that will help them to golden riches.

dry washer, they all seek a new bonanza; yet many are
willing to settle for a nugget or a few gleaming flakes.
Some are sufficiently inspired by the search itself to
continue hopefully weekend after weekend. Some
switch to other exciting pursuits or hobbies.

Many of these casual prospectors are called "snip-
ers." According to the still-active Mining Law of 1872,

59

you are allowed to explore freely on open Federal lands and keep whatever valuable minerals you find.

One drawback to sniping is that you have no more or less right to work an area than any other person. Thus, prospectors often crowd each other along a promising stretch of stream bed. An uncovered nugget may attract swarms of gold hunters to a narrow desert dry wash.

If you take your prospecting more seriously, however, the best means for protecting your interests is to stake a claim to the land you intend to work. This procedure applies to public lands only. You have no right to prospect or even trespass on privately owned property.

Before filing a claim you must research the area. You must study county records, pore over land maps, and perhaps consult library files to determine what land is still in public domain and unclaimed. You may need to check the United States Forest Service, for there are definite rules and environmental restrictions for mining on national forest lands. You can question the Bureau of Land Management or the Bureau of Mines, both agencies of the United States Department of the Interior. In all, you must do considerable homework before setting out to establish a claim.

Most importantly, before you can stake a mining

claim, you must be able to show proof that the property does, in fact, contain some valuable mineral.

To stake a claim, which may be from a few square yards up to twenty acres in size, you mark your discovery with a post at least three feet high. You survey your claim and establish its boundaries with corner posts. Then you fill out a simple location notice obtained from the county courthouse or a land management office. You file the original with the county recorder and post a duplicate in a weatherproof receptacle on the claim.

Having recorded the claim, you do not actually own the parcel of land, but it is exclusively yours to explore and reap its mineral harvest just as long as you abide by the rules. In addition to avoiding pollution and environmental damage, you must agree to do at least $100's worth of assessment work on your claim each year. Assessment work involves the actual labor in digging for gold and also includes repairing a road or performing other jobs that further the search. You must also file an annual affidavit with both the county recorder and the Federal Government that you have met the requirement. If in any year you fail to do your assessment work, the land reverts back into public domain and squatters can move in and take over where you left off.

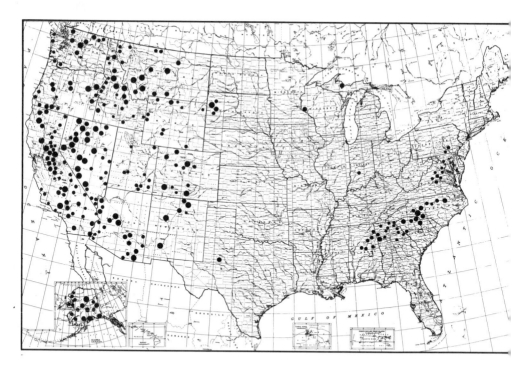

Gold is scattered widely throughout the United States—
and the world.

There is much open land throughout the United
States that is subject to claim staking. Some gold is
found in such Southern states as Tennessee and Alabama, there is more to the north along the Canadian
border. But the nation's main source of gold is in the
West. Gold occurs in placer and hardrock areas stretch-
ing from Texas to the Dakotas. It is sprinkled throughout the Rocky Mountains and spreads all the way to
the Pacific Ocean. Every Western state from Alaska

62

to Arizona, from Colorado to California, contains paying amounts of gold. All you need do is go after it.

Most amateur and quite a few professional prospectors concentrate on digging for placer gold. This kind of gold can be in the form of flakes or larger nuggets. Much of it has been battered and pulverized into a powder, often called "flour gold."

In whatever form—flake, nugget, or powder—placer gold is easiest to reach and most widely sought by a majority of prospectors. To prospect for it, you must search the low spots where the heavy fragments of gold dust finally come to rest. Be particularly alert where quartz rock is plentiful, for gold and quartz seem to go together. Study the terrain. See where the crumbling rock has washed down into stream beds, always grinding along, pulverizing itself, and dropping out its gold along the way.

Once you find color, try to choose the most likely spots where larger chunks may have settled out of the rushing stream sometime in the distant past. They are likely to be upstream from where you discovered your first powdery samples. So work your way in that direction.

Also visualize where strong spring floods that flush gold-bearing silt down ravines and stream beds may have been slowed down, giving the heavy gold a chance

Stream beds are likely spots to pan for gold.

to settle. Search the inside bend of a stream, where such slowing may have occurred. Similarly, the upstream edge of a sandbar, where the flow of the stream slows before veering off on a new course, may be a good location.

Equally promising are the pockets that eddying water hollows out on the downstream side of large

Rocky benches marking ancient stream beds
are sometimes rich with gold.

boulders or other obstructions. During the churning
action, deposits of heavy black sand or nuggets are apt
to collect in the hole. Fine gold often is found in the
black sand, or magnetite. It is important, therefore,
that you learn to read a stream.

However, placer-gold deposits certainly are not
limited to active stream beds. Waterways of all types
are forever changing their courses. They are diverted
by rock slides, earthquakes, or by the daily erosion that
steadily wears away their banks, shuffles their bottom

sand and gravel, and cuts new channels. Often the old, dried-up channels are plainly marked with rounded, water-tumbled rocks, strips of barren sand, and sparse vegetation. These high and dry benches, or terraces, may have been overlooked or ignored by earlier generations of prospectors, since locations with lots of running water were simpler to work. Hence, the dry stretches often prove more rewarding than the still-flowing but worked-over section of a creek or river.

Frequently gold comes to rest on the solid bedrock, although it also may be sprinkled through the overburden (sand, gravel, or other loose material) on top of it. If you have found signs of gold, therefore, you should explore the overburden thoroughly, whether it is two or ten feet deep, and make sure you dig far enough to reach solid bedrock. A little knowledge of geology and study of the pitch and makeup of a stream bed will help you do so.

Some successful placer mining takes place on arid deserts, where periodic cloudbursts have chipped the gold-bearing quartz from cactus-covered hills. In flash floods that may last but an hour or two, the murky waters race down wide dry washes, depositing flakes or nuggets of gold wherever curves or obstructions slow the flow. Although retrieving gold from dry sands is much more difficult than from stream-washed overburdens, a great deal of placer gold is produced in Southwest desert areas.

No matter what the locale, prospecting for gold requires preparation. You must be willing to endure hot sun, cold water, dewy nights, probably plain food, and most of all hard work.

Your basic equipment will include a good pick and a sturdy round-nosed shovel. A knife of some sort is invaluable for prying nuggets out of crevices in bed-

The gold panner's tools are simple.

rock. Metal or heavy plastic pails are well suited to transporting gold-bearing sand or gravel. Add a magnet to help separate the iron-heavy black sand from the gold. A magnifying glass and a pair of tweezers are useful for locating and lifting out small nuggets and flakes. And carry a small glass or plastic vial or two to put your treasure in.

But the most important piece of equipment is your gold pan. Gold pans come in various sizes and shapes. They generally range from ten to sixteen inches across the top, are approximately two and one half inches deep, and have broad, sloping sides that flare gradually to the rim.

Originally all such pans were made of steel. An early prospector used his pan not only to search for gold but to feed his mule, wash his shirt, or warm some leftover beans. Some steel pans are still being used today. But most modern gold pans are molded of durable, lightweight plastic. They are dyed a dark color, often deep green, against which the gold is easily visible. Most pans have built-in ridges, or riffles, that help trap the gold dust or nuggets. The most popular size is a handy fourteen-inch model.

Many variations in the art of panning gold exist, and there are devoted followers of each. But all panning is based on a single simple principle. You make

Specially constructed motorized pans are used
by some serious gold hunters.

use of gravity to separate the small amounts of heavy
precious metal from the large amounts of lighter waste
material, or overburden.

Set yourself up for panning by selecting a spot along
a stream where the running water is six inches to a
foot deep. If you are going to pan for a long time and

don't mind dangling your feet in cold water, try to find a place along the edge of the stream where you can sit comfortably on a rock or patch of dry ground. Some prefer to kneel or squat, but you may find this position tiring until you get hardened to it.

To operate the pan, fill it about two-thirds with whatever sand or gravel you are working. Submerge the pan under the water. Jiggle it back and forth vigorously to start separating the lighter overburden from the heavier sands. Work the material around with your free hand to help dissolve the dirt and clay. Let the current carry the mud away. Pick out the larger stones and cast them aside. Make a habit of examining the rocks before you get rid of them, for there just might be a shining nugget imbedded in one. Save anything that has a metallic glint. It could be silver or platinum.

Now raise the pan partly out of the water. Tilt it a little away from you, and swirl it around to help wash still more of the light overburden over the outer rim and into the stream. Be careful not to let any of the black, heavy sand go out with it. Occasionally tip the pan back toward you to resettle the heavy sand in the bottom or behind the built-in riffles.

Lift the pan completely out of the water now and then. Hold it level and shake it. Skim off still more of

Carefully flush the "heavies" out of the tilted pan.

the lighter materials. When you get it all worked down to about a half cup or so of black sand, drain off all but an inch of water. Swish it around and check the black sand on the bottom for the yellow glint of gold. If you've been lucky, you can pluck out the flakes and nuggets with your tweezers and slip them into your vial or small bottle. By all means, save the black con-

71

centrate that remains in the pan. It may contain gold dust that you can't see. You can work it down carefully later on, perhaps in the comfort of your camp.

With patience and practice, you will develop your own system of panning. You will establish a relaxed, energy-saving rhythm that will spare your muscles and hold off fatigue.

On the other hand, if you wish to speed up the process of separating gold from the overburden, you may try using a rocker. Basically, a rocker, or cradle, consists of a box, or hopper, into which you shovel the sand and gravel. Beneath the hopper is a screen made

A typical gold rocker looks and operates the same today as a hundred years ago.

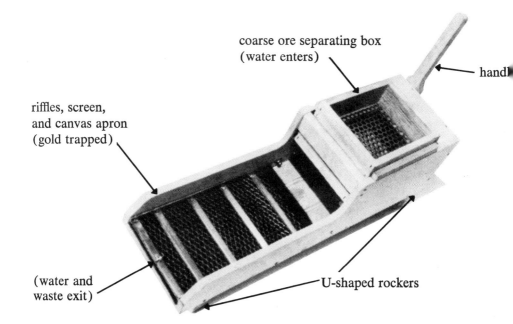

coarse ore separating box
(water enters)

handl

riffles, screen,
and canvas apron
(gold trapped)

(water and
waste exit)

U-shaped rockers

of about one half inch wire mesh. When you douse the gold-bearing material with water, the mesh retains the coarse rock while the finer sand and pebbles filter through onto a slanting canvas or carpet apron to which much of the gold from the sifted solution clings.

Below the apron is a wide, gently slanting low-sided trough about three feet long with several wooden riffles tacked across its bottom. As the sand and pebbles continue to wash down from the canvas or carpet platform, these riffles trap any gold dust or flakes that may have escaped the apron. While this process is taking place, you rock the cradle in order to increase the agitation and aid the separation of heavy from light materials.

Although a rocker can be worked by an individual, a partnership is better. Then one can keep feeding ore into the hopper while the other rocks and sloshes water into the cradle. The big advantage of rockering over panning is that several times as much sand and gravel can be worked per hour.

For prospecting on the desert, where water is either scarce or nonexistent, you must resort to dry washing. In the old days, the Mexicans and Indians simply winnowed the dry gold-bearing material by tossing it up into the air and letting the wind carry away the lighter particles, while the heavy gold settled straight down, perhaps onto a blanket. But winnowing gold is a primitive and not very successful way to prospect.

A typical modern dry washer is about the same size and can process almost as much material as a water-fed rocker. It, too, operates on the same principle of using gravity to separate heavy gold from lighter overburden.

The material you intend to run through a dry washer must be completely dry and reasonably fine. So break up chunks of clay or large pieces of conglomerate before attempting to run them through it.

Like the cradle, the dry washer is made up of a feed-in hopper, a screen-mesh sieve, and a riffle box. Instead of using water, however, the dry washer employs a bellows to blow away the overburden while the heavier minerals settle to the lowest level.

As you feed dry ore into the hopper, you vigorously use a hand crank or, better, a small motor to operate the bellows up and down. The short, strong puffs of air from the bellows blow upward through the porous canvas that forms its upper surface. Combined with the shaking of the machine, the force of the air separates the lighter materials and sends them tumbling over the riffle bars and off the end. The heavy gold sands and nuggets settle in front of the riffle bars just as they do in a water-washed rocker.

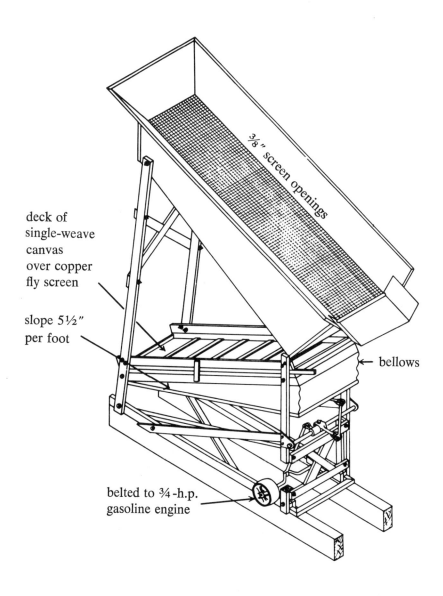

deck of
single-weave
canvas
over copper
fly screen

slope 5½″
per foot

belted to ¾-h.p.
gasoline engine

3/8″ screen openings

bellows

A dry washer uses vibration and puffs of air
to separate gold from pulverized ore.

Occasionally you must shut down to do a cleanup, plucking out the flakes or nuggets and saving whatever dark, gold-rich sand may have collected on the riffle table.

You also can dry wash by using a gold pan, particularly one of the newer types with built-in riffle traps. But any kind of dry washing is slow, dusty work, and the final refining of the collected concentrates needs to be done with water.

Thus, panning, rockering, and dry washing are three methods by which you can separate precious metals from the sands and gravels that abound in placer mining areas. If you are diligent in your search, work hard, and have a little luck—which no successful prospector will deny—you are apt to take a bit of powdered gold, a few flakes, or even a nugget or two home with you.

5

From Sluices to Sniffers

Today large numbers of both amateur and professional prospectors have returned to the century-old process of sluicing for gold. Even a small sluice box processes many times the amount of sand and gravel that can be worked with pan or rocker.

Instead of the heavy, handmade wooden sluices of the past, a modern sluice is usually small, lightweight, portable, and quite inexpensive. The most popular models are three to six feet long. They are usually made of pressed aluminum sheeting and weigh only five to ten pounds. They are easy to move around or carry in a backpack.

Basically, the sluice is a flat-bottomed trough that flares out at the input end, then quickly squeezes down to a long riffle section some eight to twelve inches wide. Laid across this section are the usual riffle bars that perform the initial separation of the ore. Beneath the riffles is a layer of screen, such as metal lath, to reduce the material further as it settles out along the sluice. And beneath it is a matting, usually a piece of short-nap carpeting, to trap the fine black sand and flecks of gold.

To set up a sluice, a person first must seek a shallow place in the stream where the current is steady and fairly swift. He lays the sluice into a bed of bottom rocks so the discharge end is slightly lower than the upstream, or feed-in, end. Then he anchors the sluice with rocks so about a two-inch-deep stream of water flows through it.

If the prospector is working sand or stream gravel, he need only shovel a little at a time into the upstream end of the sluice. The flowing water carries the lighter materials over the riffles, while the heavy, valuable concentrates are trapped by them, or sift down onto the screen or matting.

Caution must be taken that the water does not run

Set the sluice carefully in the stream's flow.

so fast through the box that it flushes the heavy, desirable materials on out with the overburden. Also one must be careful not to overload the box by feeding the sand and gravel in so fast that it clogs up. Proper techniques come with practice. Primarily, the trick is to keep a close watch and adjust the pitch of the sluice and the rate of water flow so the materials move freely yet not too swiftly through it.

As he feeds the material slowly into the sluice, the operator spreads it around with his fingers and works it over to help dissolve the dirt and clay and release whatever heavy gold might be in them. He flips out the larger rocks and lets the lighter matter wash on down the riffle section.

When the accumulation of sand and other fine material covers a good portion of the screen and matting beneath the riffle bars, it is time to do a cleanup. Then the prospector lifts the sluice from the stream bed and dismantles it piece by piece. As he raises it he keeps it level in order not to spill out any of the valuables. Slowly he sets it down on the stream bank and removes the riffle bars. Holding them over a bucket, he carefully rinses off any concentrate clinging to them. After setting the riffle bars aside, he lifts out the screening and rinses it in the bucket. At the same time, he checks for any flakes or small nuggets that might be wedged in the mesh.

Now the operator comes to the matting itself, where most of the fine gold will naturally lodge. He removes it from the sluice and rolls it gently inward. Being careful not to let anything fall from it, he slips the rolled matting into the bucket and douses it thoroughly with panfuls of water. Still keeping it poised over the bucket, he then rolls the matting in the opposite direction to

For cleanup, lift the sluice from the stream bed.

spread the nap and rinses it some more. Then, before setting the matting aside, he uses his magnifying glass and tweezers to inspect and pluck out any deeply imbedded flakes trapped in the nap.

Just to make sure he has missed nothing, the gold hunter rinses out and gathers up whatever black or shiny material may have sifted through the matting and lies inside the metal riffle box.

Remove and rinse riffles, screening, and matting,
catching all gold-rich paydirt in a bucket.

When all this work has been done, the sluice operator may find a cupful or so of the black concentrate
in the bottom of the rinsing bucket. If he is really
lucky, he may see the sheen of yellow dust sprinkled
through it. Regardless, he saves all the fine dark sand
for further examination later on when he has more

time. Then he reassembles the sluice, anchors it back in the stream, grabs his buckets, and goes after another load of promising pay dirt.

Today many serious prospectors and professionals go deep into icy cold streams to get at precious metals that heretofore have remained out of reach. They use a simple face mask and snorkel to peer down from the surface, then submerge briefly to dig out whatever looks promising. Or they use more sophisticated self-contained underwater breathing apparatus (SCUBA) gear for added efficiency. Often, instead of carrying scuba tanks on their backs, they get their breathing air through a long hose connecting their face mask and regulator to an air compressor located above water. This method is called "hookah" diving.

Besides diving equipment, they usually wear a wet suit and light boots or canvas shoes to insulate them from the cold and protect them from sharp rocks on the bottom. Also they add a safe, quick-release, weighted belt to counterbalance the thermal suit's buoyancy and enable them to work underwater.

Above all, they need a buddy for both companionship and safety. Underwater exploring is not for the loner. Nor is it for the untrained. In fact, unless the person has completed a full course of instruction and has been properly certified, he or she is not allowed to

Dredging is at least a two-person operation.

purchase scuba gear, let alone use it. And even without
cumbersome scuba tanks to contend with, hookah diving is risky and demanding.

The best time for underwater prospecting is after
heavy spring runoffs have receded and the water has
settled and cleared. Also summer's warmth will have
raised the water temperature a few degrees.

In the same manner that he would snorkel in a quiet
lagoon to observe tropical fish, the snorkeler explores

the stream searching for nature's riffles along the bottom. The most promising are the cracks and crevices in the bedrock that slice crosswise through the stream. They form natural traps for catching the fine gold or heavy nuggets that have dropped out of the fast-flowing water.

Once he locates such a crevice or other promising underwater deposit, the diver submerges. With knife blade or pointed rock hammer, he pries out whatever he can reach. Or he may use a sniffer, a sort of over-sized medicine dropper, to suck up the deeper-lying gold-bearing concentrate.

Surfacing frequently to put his findings in a jar or pail for later refining, the diver moves upstream from crack to crevice. Also he explores where swirling eddies may have stacked up gold-bearing sand and gravel under the downstream edge of boulders. He checks around any obstruction that may have slowed the water flow and given the heavy metal-rich material an opportunity to settle out.

These days many professional gold seekers combine diving with dredging. More than ever, a team effort is needed. In order to spread out expenses, ensure safety, and share the excitement, enjoyment, and profits, if any, such ventures lend themselves to group participation and support. Scuba gear and wet suits are expensive. And a portable gold dredge runs from hundreds into thousands of dollars.

The size and variety of portable gold dredges are endless. Some are homemade. Many are produced by both small and large mining equipment manufacturers scattered coast to coast across the United States.

Basically, the gold dredge is made up of a suction pump run by a small gasoline engine. The pump attaches to a flexible vinyl hose that may be from two

A portable gold dredge is basically
a motorized suction pump, a long vacuum hose,
and a riffle table mounted on some type of float.

to six inches in diameter, depending upon the size
of the dredge and the amount of power available.
Mounted on the dredge is a riffle-barred sluice, similar
to but larger than most common sluice boxes. If scuba
tanks are not used by the diver, breathing air is provided by a hookah compressor also mounted on the
dredge and fed to the diver through a long hose.

All of this equipment is set atop some kind of a
flotation system. Perhaps it is simply a large inflated
truck inner tube. Or the apparatus may be carried in
a small boat. More often than not, it is mounted on
hollow pontoons of one design or another. All parts

should be easy to dismantle, for very often the dredge has to be carried piece by piece and reassembled in some remote but promising canyon far from a convenient road. '

With everything in order, both hookah diver and partner get into wet suits. While one dives, the other works the dredge. With the suction pump motor and the air pump operating, the diver hooks the bright yellow, highly visible breathing hose to his mask. The hose is buoyant, so any surplus rises toward the surface, preventing the diver from getting tangled in the trailing coils.

The team sets up a safety signal system. Perhaps a single tug on the hose or on a special line indicates that all is fine below. Several quick jerks might signal trouble, or "pull me up." Whatever system is agreed upon for keeping in touch with each other, the partners use the system frequently as the work progresses.

With the dredge functioning, the diver submerges, taking the open end of the suction hose to the bottom with him. He systematically searches for crevices or hollows where loose sand and gravel have collected. Brushing away the lighter overburden with a gloved hand and letting the current carry it downstream, he works down to the finer sand, then moves the end of the hose unhurriedly across it. When all the easy-to-reach loose material has been vacuumed up, the diver takes his rock pick, knife, or other crevice tool and digs out the fine materials or flakes and nuggets of gold wedged deeper down in the crack where the suction hose hasn't reached.

With everything operating properly, the only limit to the time the diver can stay down is perhaps the coldness of the water. Although wet suit, gloves, and boots keep the diver fairly snug for a while, the chill of the cold water is bound to get to him before long. So the best procedure is to keep the dives fairly short and trade off regularly with a partner or partners.

Meanwhile, whoever remains on the surface operates the sluice. It is important that he keeps the floating equipment fairly level so the pumped-up material flows steadily, neither too slow nor too fast, through the riffled section. He controls the water flow to a mild bubbling boil so the overburden tumbles along, dropping out the heavy valuables before it reaches the tail end. Periodically, as with any gold-separating equipment, the dredge must be shut down for a careful cleanup.

Prospecting for gold with a floating dredge has opened up entirely new areas of exploration. Indeed, modest fortunes have been made with one. However, in many areas there are local, state, or Federal laws

While one partner works underwater,
the other tends the dredge.

governing their use. Often they are tied in with con-
servation and antipollution regulations. Sometimes
dredging, like hunting and fishing, is restricted to certain locations and certain seasons. Gold hunters must
check these things out before starting to prospect.

During recent years many prospectors have turned
to electronic-age equipment to improve their chances
of locating precious metals. Battery-powered metal de-

tectors have become increasingly popular in the search for gold. Developed from wartime land-mine detectors, the sensitive modern devices are being used for all kinds of treasure hunting. Beachcombers locate watches, rings, coins, and metallic objects lost in the sand with them. Others use them to probe around ghost towns, school yards, or parks for buried or hidden objects. Indeed, electronic sleuthing is a widespread activity with a growing number of followers.

The same techniques and electronic detectors used to search for coins can be adopted for gold prospecting. A detector sounds or flashes its signal as readily for a gold nugget buried in the sand of a riverbed as for a musket ball hidden in the soil of some historic battlefield.

The searching disc, or loop, of the detector does not sniff out loosely scattered gold dust. However, it will expose concentrations of heavy metallic sand that may contain the fine gold. Thus, detectors are widely used for ferreting out deposits of black metal-rich sand that may lie at the bottom of a shallow stream.

Generally, a piece of gold needs to be somewhat bigger than a carpet tack in order to trigger an electronic signal in the detector. Even then the prospector may find his quarry to be nothing more than a rusty nail. However, newer detectors have built-in discrim-

An electronic detector sniffs out nuggets
that might otherwise be passed over.

inators to tune out tinfoil, bottle caps, small nails, aluminum pull tabs, wire, and most other bothersome junk metal.

Metal detectors can be used effectively in areas where nuggets are known to have been found or in old mines where they might detect a hidden vein not reached before. In Australia, tremendous nuggets weighing up to forty-five pounds have been located by such detectors.

In any event, whether sluicers, dredgers, or sniffers are used, there is certainly more gold to be found.

6

Gold at Work

One of the reasons that gold is so valuable is its scarcity. It is estimated that if all the known pure gold ever mined were gathered in one place, it would weigh less than 90,000 tons and would pack into a single cube measuring about fifty-four feet to a side. That is hardly enough to fill a medium-sized barn.

Once separated from the ore, gold is refined and processed into powder, granules, foil, wire, sheets, rods, bars, or in ingots weighing up to four hundred ounces. Some gold exists in pure form, mostly as raw material

A refinery worker pours pure gold from a smelter pot.

Granules and ingots are two of the many forms of gold.

or bullion. But pure gold is too soft for practical use in industry or the arts. So, before being used, most of it is diluted into harder alloys with other metals such as silver, copper, nickel, or zinc. Such alloy metals also tint the gold in varying shades of yellow, green, pink, red, or white.

Gold's purity is expressed in units called "karats" (or "carats"), broken down into fractions of twenty-fourths. Therefore, 24-karat gold is pure gold. Another unit used is called "fine," which measures the proportion of pure gold in an alloy, the maximum being a thousand. Thus, pure 24-karat gold is also 1000 fine.

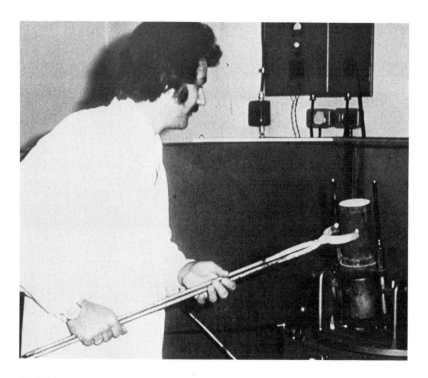

Gold is assayed to determine its purity.

Actually, a little leeway is allowed, and any gold that is at least 99.5 percent clean—or 995 fine—is ranked as pure or fine gold.

Gold stamped *18k* is eighteen parts of gold mixed with six parts of other metals. Thus, it is 75 percent pure or 750 fine. The 14-karat alloy commonly used in American jewelry is a little better than 58 percent gold. In modern inflationary times, 14-karat jewelry has largely given way to a further diluted 12-karat alloy. A wise shopper keeps alert to the stamped karat

The purity of a bar of gold is expressed in karats.

rating in order not to pay more than the item is worth. In the United States, any article that can legally be labeled as gold must be at least 10-karat or 10-24ths gold.

Gold is weighed according to the troy system instead of avoirdupois. There are 480 grains to a troy ounce, compared to 437 grains in an ounce avoirdupois. So the troy ounce is slightly heavier. Due to its great density, one cubic inch of gold weighs about ten troy ounces, or nearly a pound. A cubic foot, a mere pailful, weighs about half a ton.

In addition to the larger items of bullion, such as bars or ingots, gold coins of assorted sizes and shapes have been minted for more than two thousand years. The United States stopped minting gold coins in 1934, and virtually all of the famous twenty-dollar double eagle coins that still remain of the more than 174 million that were minted over an eighty-year period are in the hands of coin collectors (numismatists) or tucked away in strongboxes.

Then, in 1980, the United States Government once again started issuing limited quantities of gold for sale to the public. It is now available in the form of a half-ounce, round gold medallion honoring famed singer Marian Anderson and a one-ounce version featuring American artist Grant Wood. At gold's current price, most of these medallions undoubtedly will also end up in collections or safes.

Many other countries mint coins, medallions, wafers, or small bars of pure gold bullion for public sale. Great

Gold coins and medallions have long been bartered
or collected throughout the world.

Britain, Austria, Hungary, Canada, Mexico, Switzerland, and others mint such items in various weights and denominations. South Africa, which mines approximately 700 tons of gold annually, is by far the world's largest producer. And the South African Krugerrand, round bullion coins that come in several sizes, have long been favored by collectors.

In these various forms, gold simply represents wealth. How secure the wealth is depends upon the constantly fluctuating price of gold, and those who deal in it take that risk.

Gold's more practical value, however, lies in its many uses. Large amounts of gold are consumed by industry. Being noncorrosive and having excellent properties for conducting electricity, gold is widely used in sensitive electronic devices. A very thin film of gold can carry the same electrical load that once required cumbersome wiring. Thus, largely through the use of small, gold-printed circuit boards and pinhead-sized silicon chips, microminiaturization developed. Such gold-aided circuitry is found in all types of solid-state electronics, from adding machines to computers to television sets.

Having excellent reflective qualities, thin gold foil covered the Apollo spacecraft to protect it from solar heat. Gold coatings on the astronauts' faceplates

Much gold is used in microminiature electronic circuitry
for space-age hardware such as satellites.

shielded them from harmful rays during their explorations of the moon. Much gold also is used in the space shuttle system.

This reflective value is why the windows in some large office buildings are coated with a thin, see-through film of gold. Without hampering visibility, the gold deflects the sun's heat and cuts down on the amount of air conditioning needed.

A most malleable metal in its pure form, gold can

The reflective properties of gold protect astronauts from harmful solar rays.

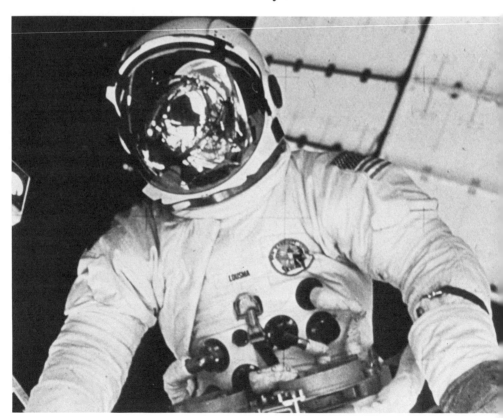

be pounded into a leaf so thin that about 250,000 would make a stack only an inch high. Either in the form of gold leaf, or stirred into an oily paintlike mixture, gold is used for all sorts of labeling. Signs on office doors and store windows are crafted of gold leaf. Gold-leaf lettering and designs are stamped onto high-quality books. Thin gold paints are used in millions of perfume bottles to add an aura of luxury. Some of the finest cloth materials are interwoven with gold thread. Industrial uses for gold are ever-widening.

However, due to its enormously increased cost, industry is seeking metallic substitutes. Nickel, chromium, copper, manganese, and tin are among many metals being tested in alloys. Silver and platinum, precious metals themselves, are often used in place of gold. But they, too, are costly. And no other metal or alloy has yet been found to possess all of the desired characteristics of gold. In many instances, the answer to high cost is to use thinner microcoatings while trying to retain the same quality and efficiency. To a large degree, through improved metallurgical processes such as gold electroplating, this solution is working.

For generations, large amounts of gold have been used in dentistry. Being a stable metal that doesn't tarnish and is little affected by acids or temperature changes, gold is particularly suitable for dental crowns, inlays, fillings, and bridgework. But at today's prices, the use of gold in dentistry is becoming excessively expensive. And although much gold still is being worked with, many patients settle for less permanent alloys such as silver. There is a constant search for gold substitutes in dentistry.

Gold has been found to have medicinal value. For half a century, injections of soluble gold salts have proven beneficial in the treatment of rheumatoid arthritis. And injections of solutions containing small amounts of radioactive gold are used for treating certain types of cancer. Being chemically inert and, therefore, not affected by body fluids, gold often is helpful in eye surgery involving the transplantation of optical parts. Research is constantly under way for new ways that gold can serve medicine.

Much of the gold that goes into industry and dentistry is salvaged and used over and over again. Discarded electronic parts and other gold scrap is refined and recycled back into gold-bearing products. Broken or outgrown dental bridges are melted down and worked again. Some metal is lost or discarded in gold plating, but most gold is reclaimed and, in one form or another, continues a long life. As prices continue to rise, the reclamation efforts become increasingly helpful.

Most of the gold that is not held as some form of investment or used by industry, dentistry, or medicine appears in jewelry or in other forms of a goldsmith's art. It may be worked into a ring or a simple pair of cuff links. Possibly a natural nugget as it was originally plucked from the ground may be worn as a pendant. Plain gold neck chains or chains combined with some sort of charm or religious amulet are popular for both men and women. More gold is used for school rings than for any other type of jewelry. A golden brooch or a bracelet set with precious or semiprecious gems is usually preferred to an ounce or two of gold bullion tucked away in some safe-deposit box.

A skilled goldsmith prepares a mold to produce a nest of rings.

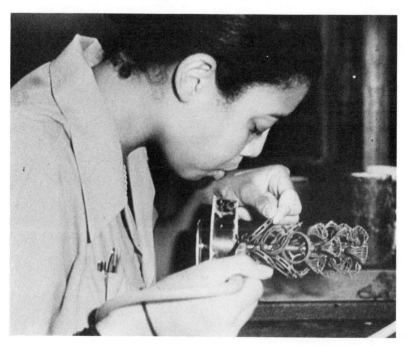

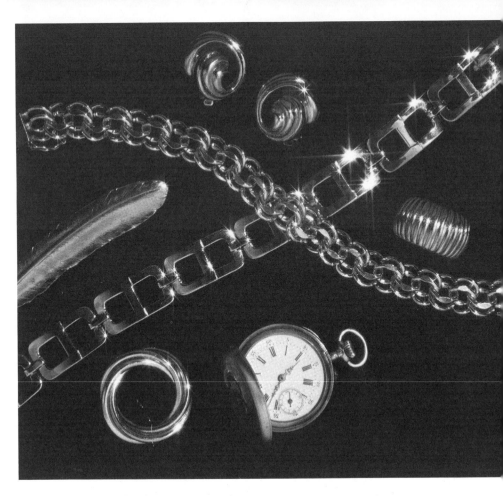

The world's most favored jewelry is made of gold.

So the making and wearing of jewelry and the crafting of it into other items such as statuettes, pens, lighters, tableware, and various decorative items account for the major consumption of gold, about 50 percent of the total.

In order to make products more affordable to all, many so-called gold items are actually gold-overlaid or gold-filled. These objects are made of some base metal or alloy, such as copper or brass, and merely coated with gold. However, any article marked gold-filled must have a bonded gold covering that makes up not less than 1-20th of the item's total weight and be at least 10-karat fine.

Much high-quality costume jewelry is made of "rolled gold plate," which is similar to gold-filled jewelry except that the gold layer is less than 1-20th of the total weight.

Other less-expensive jewelry and decorative items are electrolytically coated with a very thin skin of gold. If labeled at all, such articles may be marked "gold washed" or "gold flashed." Although pleasing to the eye, they are not noted for their gold content or their resistance to wear.

Yet whether an object is solid 24-karat pure, a 14-karat alloy, or is simply a thin electroplated coating spread over a cheap metal foundation, people are still drawn to gold, Earth's most noble metal.

7

Silver and Platinum

The idea of calling certain metals "precious" was originated by jewelers. First the classification applied only to gold and silver, since they were the most handsome, noncorrosive, durable, and easy to work of the known metals. Not until the mideighteenth century—about two hundred years after its initial discovery by Spanish conquerors—was platinum added to the small group of precious metals.

For a while, the superior metals were used primarily by artistic craftsmen. Next to gold, silver was the most

108

desirable. Many of its properties were similar to those of gold. Although harder than gold, silver is sufficiently malleable to be easily molded, shaped, or hammered into leaf so thin that light shines through it. Being ductile, it can be drawn out into almost invisibly fine wire.

Soft ductile silver is drawn through dies
into assorted sizes of wire.

Polished silver also has a bright moonbeam glow that makes it most pleasing to the eye. Like gold, silver resists corrosion and is unaffected by moisture, vegetable acids, or alkalis. Its prime drawback is that its exterior surfaces tarnish black when exposed to the sulfur that, at least to a small degree, is ever present in the air. Thus, unlike gold, silver must be periodically polished to retain its shine.

Silver is mined throughout the world, with major production in Canada, Mexico, Peru, Russia, and the United States. Lesser amounts are mined in Germany, Spain, South Africa, Japan, and Australia.

A small amount of silver is gleaned from placer

Major and minor sources of silver
are scattered around the world.

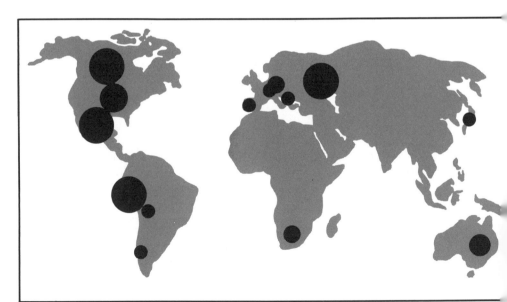

Silver and platinum, as well as gold, emerge as by-products from this enormous open pit copper mine in Utah.

operations. Most, however, comes from underground mines. Sometimes it occurs in almost pure lodes. But more often than not it is found in ores that also contain lead, copper, gold, or other metals. Seldom, in fact, does any metal, base or precious, emerge alone. Almost always it is mixed with other elements.

Being somewhat harder than gold, silver is durable enough to be used in its pure form. The fine, or sterling, silver used in high-quality artworks, jewelry, or tableware is at least 925 parts of silver to 75 parts copper. As is true of gold, the price of silver has skyrocketed during the past years; sterling jewelry, tea sets, tableware, and ornaments have become increasingly scarce and certainly more costly.

Silver is very often alloyed with copper, lead, mer-

At a refinery silver crystals are harvested from special processing cells.

Silver crystals go into a casting furnace.

cury, or other metals to make it less expensive. Or an electroplated silver coating is applied over a base metal core. Today, most people are usually willing to accept the less expensive but equally handsome alloyed or plated items.

113

But long ago jewelry and artworks ceased being the main products of silver. Stainless steel, aluminum, and other nonprecious metal alloys are increasingly being substituted for silver in many items such as table flatware, mirrors, and surgical supplies. Silver has all but disappeared from coinage around the world. It has been replaced by nickel, copper, brass, and other base metal combinations.

Industry now consumes at least two-thirds of the world's annual output of silver. About a third of all the silver used in the United States goes into photography. Indeed, the very essence of photography is based on the fact that certain salts of silver are sensitive to the action of light. Thus, both the film and the processing use vast amounts of silver converted to crystalline salts. Fortunately, some of this silver can be reclaimed from solutions and reused. But it is still the most costly of photographic materials. Searches for silver substitutes in photography have been partially successful and are constantly being pursued. In time, great amounts of the precious metal will be freed for other industrial uses.

Being the best-known conductor of heat and electricity, silver is widely used in electrical switches and appliances and for other electronic purposes. Yet the rising price of silver has prompted the substitution of

Photography film and printing papers
depend upon the use of silver in the form
of light-sensitive silver nitrates.

less-efficient but also less-costly metals such as copper.

Batteries that once consumed substantial amounts of silver are being replaced by newer power cells that use the reactions of hydrogen and oxygen combinations to generate electricity. In another area industry consumes large amounts of silver to bond or braze metal alloys that will not respond properly to other types of adhesives such as solder. There are, indeed, hundreds of little-known ways silver is used by industry.

Much the same can be said for platinum, even more

115

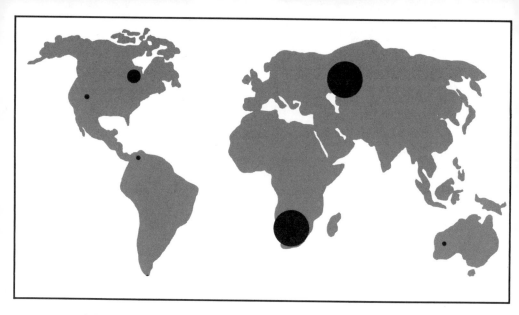

Most platinum is produced
in Russian, South African, and Canadian mines.

rare and expensive than gold. Actually, six separate
yet similar metals make up the so-called platinum
group. They are platinum and palladium, which together account for about 94 percent of the platinum
metal mined. The others are rhodium (3 percent),
ruthenium (2 percent), and iridium and osmium (approximately 1 percent combined). For convenience,
and since the differences in their properties are relatively small, this group of gray-white, highly valued
metals is referred to simply as platinum.

Platinum often is found in gold-bearing ores and at
times has been called "white gold" for its cool luster.

116

But flakes and grains of it also are found in nickel, copper, and lead ores. Additional platinum emerges as a by-product from the refining of nickel, copper, gold, or silver, where it is chemically extracted from the so-called slimes that form during the complicated processing of pulverized metal-rich ores. Rarely is platinum discovered isolated from other base or precious metals. It is not frequently found in nugget form, although some small amounts of platinum come from hand-worked placer operations.

Although to a lesser degree than silver and gold, platinum is ductile and easy to work. It resists corro-

Filtering drums separate precious metals from slurried ore concentrates.

sion and does not tarnish as silver does in the presence of sulfur traces. It is affected only by a combination of nitric and hydrochloric acids, known as aqua regia, which even dissolves gold.

Although the youngest of precious metals to join the family, platinum quickly became popular with jewelers. Since it combines readily with other metals, jewelers alloy it with gold, silver, nickel, or tungsten to make the strong, hard, white-hued gem setting sometimes preferred to gold.

Like gold and silver, platinum is also suited to a variety of electronic uses such as thermostats, relays, printed circuits, and all sorts of appliances. Its relatively high melting point of 3,224 degrees Fahrenheit makes it particularly suitable for lining jet engines, fabricating retorts or chemical stills, manufacturing spark plugs and many other items that must be heat-resistant.

Platinum is widely used in dentistry and medicine too. Combined with dental gold alloys, it adds strength to orthodontic devices and alters the brightly golden color to a lighter, less-noticeable hue.

In medicine, various alloys of the platinum group are used to make strong hypodermic needles and heat-resistant instrument tips for cauterizing. Being impervious to the chemical reaction of body liquids, platinum often provides the cases for cardiac pacemakers that must be implanted under the skin. Complex platinum salts are effective in the treatment of certain cancers through chemotherapy.

But by far the greatest use being made of platinum in the modern world is as a catalyst to promote chemical changes. By definition, a catalyst is an agent that, when brought in the presence of or added to something else, causes a chemical change in that something without itself undergoing a change. Thus, a catalyst usually can serve over and over, a fortunate circumstance considering the high price of platinum.

Platinum is used in catalytic converters
to cleanse automotive exhaust gases of poisonous fumes.

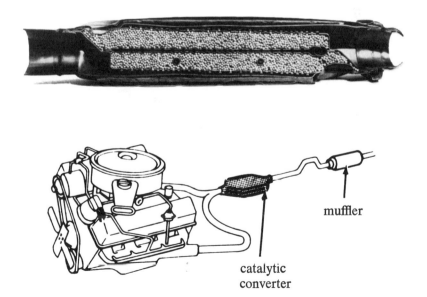

muffler

catalytic
converter

Most platinum consumed today goes into the exhaust systems of American automobiles. In combination, platinum and its close cousin palladium form such a powerful catalyst that only about five hundredths of an ounce is needed in an exhaust system to reduce the carbon-monoxide gases and hydrocarbons that are major causes of destructive smog. Such catalytic converters are required in states or areas where air pollution is a problem.

Other industries that employ platinum are glass making, oil refining, ceramic, pharmaceutical, and chemical.

Thus, gold, silver, and platinum are justly considered highest-quality metals. Not only do they beautify, they serve people in almost infinite ways.

They are, indeed, the grandest and most precious metals.

Glossary

adit—passage driven into side of hill to reach into a mine.
Ag—chemical symbol for silver, from Latin *argentum.*
alloy—a mixture of two or more metals.
amalgam—alloy of mercury with one or more other metals.
assay—to analyze a metal to determine its purity and value.
Au—chemical symbol for gold, from *aurum,* Latin for "gold."
base metal—any of the common nonprecious metals.
bedrock—solid rock beneath loose surface of ground.
black sand—mixture of heavy dark minerals and metals.
bonanza—especially rich find of precious metals.
bullion—pure gold in ingots, bars, or wafers.
claim—parcel of land legally held for mining purposes.
colors—small particles of visible gold.

121

concentrate—metal-rich material when most waste matter has been eliminated.

cradle—*see* rocker.

crevicing—prying gold from cracks or crevices with bladed instrument.

cyanidation—using sodium cyanide to extract gold or silver from ore.

diggings—location of mining activity.

drift—horizontal tunnel branching from main shaft.

ductile—ability to be stretched or drawn out into thin wire.

electroplating—process of coating an object with a thin layer of metal.

face—surface of mine being worked on.

fineness—proportion of gold in an alloy, expressed in thousandths. 750 fine equals 75 percent gold.

flour gold—gold dust.

fool's gold—brittle iron pyrite sometimes mistaken for gold.

gallows frame—*see* headframe.

gold—(chemical symbol *Au*) most ductile, malleable, and one of the heaviest of all metals.

gold leaf—gold pounded to superthinness.

grubstake—to supply a prospector with his needs for a share of his findings.

hardrock—dense, strongly bonded rock structure.

headframe—structure atop shaft housing hoisting machinery.

hookah—diving for gold with breathing apparatus.

karat (sometimes carat)—gold purity expressed in 24ths. 18k equals 75 percent gold.

lode—a vein or pocket of mineral-rich material.

metallurgy—method used to extract precious metal from soil or rock.

mill—plant where ore is ground and precious metals extracted.

mother lode—the source of placer gold.

mucking—loading loose ore after blasting.

ore—rock containing profitable amounts of metal.

overburden—layer of earth and rock covering metal-rich deposit.

patent—once-public land deeded to miner who has proved its mineral or metal worth.

pay dirt—rich, gold-containing placer findings.

placer gold—loose or free gold.

platinum—(chemical symbol *Pt*) white precious metal of dull luster; heaviest of the precious metals.

precious metals—basically gold, silver, and platinum.

Pt—chemical symbol for platinum, from Spanish *platina*.

quartz—rock composed of silica and oxygen; often gold bearing.

riffles—cross-obstructions to trap gold in separating devices.

rocker—portable sluice that rocks to hasten gold washing.

shaft—vertical or inclined mine hole.

silver—(chemical symbol *Ag*) a white, ductile, malleable metal.

sluice—riffled trough for washing placer gold ore.

sniffer—suction syringe for sucking gold from cracks or crevices.

sniping—part-time prospecting on unclaimed land.

sourdough—a veteran prospector.

sponge—an amalgam of gold and mercury.

station—room excavated along main shaft for men, machinery, and materials.

stope—working face of mine. Room.

tailings(gangue)—mine waste.

troy ounce—traditional gold measure; equals 1.097 ounces avoirdupois.

winnowing—dry placer mining by blowing away waste material.

winze—a subsidiary mine shaft that starts and ends underground, usually connecting different working levels.

Index

125

About the Author

Charles (Chick) Coombs graduated from the University of California, at Los Angeles, and decided at once to make writing his career. While working at a variety of jobs, he labored at his typewriter early in the morning and late at night. An athlete at school and college, Mr. Coombs began by writing sports fiction. He soon broadened his interests, writing adventure and mystery stories, and factual articles as well. When he had sold over a hundred stories, he decided to try one year of full-time writing, chiefly for young people, and the results justified the decision.

Eventually he turned to writing books. To date he has published more than sixty books, both fiction and nonfiction, covering a wide range of subjects, from aviation and space, to oceanography, drag racing, motorcycling, and many others. He is also author of the Be a Winner series of books explaining how various sports are played and how to succeed in them.

Mr. Coombs and his wife, Eleanor, live in Westlake Village, near Los Angeles.